MESSAGES FROM GOD
A Gift of Poetry from the Holy Spirit

Gayla Dewan Hood

Copyright © 2008 by Gayla Dewan Hood

Messages From God
A Gift of Poetry from the Holy Spirit
by Gayla Dewan Hood

Printed in the United States of America

ISBN 978-1-60647-446-4

All rights reserved solely by the author. The author guarantees all contents are original and do not infringe upon the legal rights of any other person or work. No part of this book may be reproduced in any form without the permission of the author. The views expressed in this book are not necessarily those of the publisher.

Unless otherwise indicated, Bible quotations are taken from the King James Version of the Bible. Copyright © 1970 by Crusade Bible Publishers, Inc.

www.xulonpress.com

For my family, friends and especially my grandchildren

I love you all, so much.

Contents

Preface vii

CHAPTER ONE
Inspiration 9

From the Cross 11
Answered Prayers 13
Tyler's First Smile 17
Do You Believe in Miracles? 19
The Stranger 21
Death 23
Only God 25

CHAPTER TWO
Lessons 27

Where are the Commandments? 29
Too Much To Do 31
Always One Witness 33
To Be a Little Child 35
The Lasting Book 37

CHAPTER THREE
Prophecy **39**

The Return 41
Mother Earth 43
False Prophets 45
Final Warning 47
My Children 49
Where is Peace? 51
Revelations 53
The Antichrist 55
Judgment Day 57

CHAPTER FOUR
Comfort **59**

The Day We Meet 61
All Dressed Up 63
A Gift from God 65
Your Friend 67
The Mighty Hand 69
Thank You for the Children 71
I Looked Up 73

CHAPTER FIVE
Strength **75**

Gold Watch and Chain 77
Angels Unaware 79
Open Heart 81
Get Behind Me Satan 83
Do You Ever Pray? 85

Preface

When words began to fill my head, I thought it was a fleeting moment. Little did I know, it would still be happening twenty eight years later. Believe me, I was not a poet or an author of any sort. I am a cosmetologist by trade. I had a very normal life and the mother of one son named Gary. He was four years old when this all began.

It was on a Sunday that this journey of self-discovery started. A good friend of mine, by the name of Sandra invited me to go to church with her. It would be my first church attendance in many years. The message was glorious that day, as it spoke of the gifts of the Holy Spirit. I was one, among many who listened patiently to the service that day. Just like everyone else, I was wondering what my gift was because the minister said that we all had one.

I remember thinking that maybe he's not talking to me. A few moments later he pointed out to the congregation that there was someone not getting up to come forward. At that moment, I looked up from my prayer and saw a few other people going toward the altar. Again, he said to the crowd that someone is going to miss a Holy Gift because they will not get up and come forward. I looked towards him and his gaze met mine. I knew then, he was speaking of me.

I started to feel the pull at my heart as I battled the urge to get up or stay in my seat. Get up or stay there, then almost immediately I rose to my feet and started down the isle. I knew then, it was out of my control. I kneeled at the front of the church and others joined me in prayer. I knew something had happened at church that day.

I didn't question the experience. I had faith and waited. Then, four days later on a Thursday evening during my drive home from work the Holy Spirit started telling me what to write. There I was with no paper and no pen. I tried so hard to keep the words together until I arrived home. I ran in the house and wrote what I heard. This gift that the Lord gave me has never stopped. Within five days I had written around twenty-five poems and songs.

Do you think it was a coincidence? Do you think going to church that day was my own will? I knew God had a purpose to give me this gift, of course. I also knew He would lead me to publish my poetry when He was ready. All of these years, I only listened and wrote. He's ready now.

CHAPTER ONE

Inspiration

Messages From God

When I wrote *From the Cross*, I was confused at first because it was the first message that had come to me in the first person. I remember questioning if I was hearing it correctly. I tried to rearrange the word to make it past tense but, I could not. Then after several attempts, I realized the Hold Spirit was the one talking. I was only repeating what he was saying. So, another beautiful poem was born.

This poem is perhaps the most beloved one of all by my family and friends. I know it will touch your heart as well.

FROM THE CROSS

I'm thirsty and I'm hungry. The pain only grows.
I have not done anything wrong, but I suffer so.

My blood is flowing to the ground. How long
will I survive this torture and this misery
before I finally die?

The crowd has gathered around me.
I hear them laugh and sing.
They tell me to come on down, if I'm really the King.

They're foolish for not knowing
that what I've said is true. So Father, please forgive them,
for they not know what they do.

They've driven nails in my hands
and feet and thorns upon my head.
and when I ask for water, they give vinegar instead.

But yet I love each one of them,
though pain is all they give.
They don't know I'm hanging here
so that they may live.

Father, it is finished. My life on earth is through.
I'm ready to end this torture and come live with You.

Then, the ground began to quake
and crowd began to run.
And when they saw the sky grow dark,
they knew they'd killed God's Son.

But, the pain had left our Jesus.
His wounds were now all well.
Though His body was hanging there,
His spirit in Heaven dwelled.

But, He returned to show a few
that he had risen and was not dead.
Then he ascended up to Heaven, just like He had said.

ANSWERED PRAYERS

Within our minds lies mystery. Within our hearts lies fear.
Within our lives lies destiny, but the road is never clear.

So, we worry about this and we worry about that,
    until confusion fills our souls.
Then the road we're to take just disappears
and it's impossible to know where to go.

In the midst of our troubles, so blind that we cannot see.
    Our ears hear a voice that says;
        why don't you come to Me?

At first, we think we've imagined it,
    for there's no one standing there.
We look around in amazement and the voice says;
    I've heard your prayers.

It's not that I've forgotten you and left you in battle alone,
    it's just, my child you don't obey.
    That's why your worries aren't gone.

For I know your heart is trouble
    because you talk to me now and then.
But your Lord is very busy
because this world is filled with sin.

So, for the ones of you who want to find,
    but seldom do you seek.
    I must teach you a lesson,
    until you decide to come to Me.

Then when you're so desperate
that I hear your cries from My throne,
that's when I know you're serious
and your burdens will be gone.

So, speak to me from the depth of your heart
and I will always take the time.
You give Me the best you've got,
only then, will I give you mine.

Tyler was diagnosed with spinal meningitis on June 6, 1998. He was just eight months old. He was comatose for three days and we were told that he would probably not make it through the night. Also, we were told that if he did make it that he would never be the same. On the third day he opened his eyes and smiled. This smile inspired me to write this poem for him. Our prayers were answered nine days later when he returned home from the hospital. Tyler is now in college and healthy as ever.

TYLER'S FIRST SMILE

I'd like to thank my doctor and my nurses too,
for taking such good care of me and knowing what to do.

I'd like to thank my mom and dad for staying by my side.
I know that they've been worried because I heard them cry.

But, the one I want to thank the most is
the one nobody has seen.
That's my guardian angel
who has been laying right here with me.

He's the one who sang me lullabies
that no one else could hear
and the one who gave me comfort
and took away my fears.

He was the voice inside my little head
that said I'd be alright.
He was the one who held me through the darkest night.

Though no one ever saw him, I knew that he was there,
protecting me like no one else
and showing how much he cared.

That is why I smiled today when I opened my little eyes
cause I saw my guardian angel fly back into the sky.

DO YOU BELIEVE IN MIRACLES?

Do you believe in miracles? If so, why do you fret?
You know the mighty hand of God isn't finished yet.

Sometimes our faith is tested and it seems too much to bear.
If we're strong in believing, then our Lord is always there.

Through faith, our hearts are lifted.
Through faith, we do God's will.
Through faith, we find all answers.
Through faith, we can be healed.

The Devil tries to steal away our smiles and give us tears.
When we think that all is good, the devil interferes.

He wants to make us weak in faith and pull from our Lord.
That's when we must do our best and seek Him even more.

If we feel defeated, we must not give in.
Because even if we fight till death,
a victory shall we win.

So, when the storm clouds gather
and the sunshine is far from sight,
remember what our Jesus said, that He is the light.

The Stranger is about six years old. I remember the morning God gave it to me. Someone close to me came home telling me about a man on the side of the road asking for money. I asked him if he gave and he said no.

This troubled my heart and I pleaded my cause but, this person stood firm. He replied that he would have taken him to eat all he wanted. He couldn't give someone money when he didn't know their intentions.

So I began to question, who was right? The Holy Spirit took me over as He had so many times before. What you are about to read was the answer he gave me. I know you've asked yourself this question before.

THE STRANGER

Years ago, one Christmas Eve while driving along the road,
I saw the figure of a man with his back against the cold.

In this hand he held a sign that said; I will work for food,
I'm homeless and hungry and I need some help from you.

So, I stopped and rolled the window down.
He walked over to the car.
His ragged clothes and tender smile
began to melt my heart.

I told him to come inside and warm himself a while.
He stared at me with loving eyes and said;
God bless you, child.

I took him home to feed him
and gathered him some clothes.
I offered him a place to rest but,
he insisted that he must go.

But first I must tell you;
all day long I've read people's minds.
They've passed me by, warm and happy.
Saying he only wants some wine.

He's probably a drunk and he's lazy.
Let him get a job like me.
But, your heart was understanding,
you only saw someone in need.

Then the man began to change
from his head down to his feet.
I stared in total amazement
and shook my head in disbelief.

A crown of thorns appeared
and a robe of scarlet and white.
A glow began to fill the room
and I covered my eyes from the light.

He held out his hand and touched me
and I looked up into his eyes.
I began to shake and tremble and He said,
remember this night.

Tell your friends and your family,
all your neighbors and everyone you meet.
Be careful what they say about others
for you never know what's underneath.

Tell them what they missed by passing this stranger by.
Tell them you didn't feed a beggar,
you had supper with the Lord tonight.

DEATH

Death is such an enemy. Death is hated so,
but really death is just a rest or sleep we all must know.

Why is death so hated? Why is death so feared?
If we knew that blessed peace, we'd never shed a tear.

Graves, they seem so lonely and dark, while we are alive.
But, really graves are empty, just the body lies inside.

The body is a temple that our soul lives in.
When that temple has been used enough,
God takes our soul again.

Then that's when we realize the gift our good Lord gives,
to know a last we're finally home and will forever live.

So, when you think of dreaded death
and your heart gets sad,
just remember that our precious Lord
gives nothing that is bad.

ONLY GOD

Only God knows everything. Only God can see
what lies down the road ahead. Just God knows, not me.

Only God can hold my hand and walk each step with me.
Only God can know what's best, whatever it may be.

Only God can understand how, when and why.
All the answers in the world, just God has, not I.

Only God can comfort me and ease my worried mind.
Only God will be my friend when others I can't find.

Only God can help me through the darkest night.
Only God can do great things and make all wrongs a right.

Yes, only God knows everything and only He can be
everything that's perfect and I know He lives in me.

CHAPTER TWO

Lessons

WHERE ARE THE COMMANDMENTS?

Where are the Ten Commandments
that God gave us long ago?
I guess you fell the same as I,
the answer we don't know.

Love your neighbor as yourself, has no meaning anymore.
Do not kill and do not steal,
from our hearts they have been torn.

Honor thy Father and Mother,
is something of the past and
if you don't commit adultery,
some think you have no class.

Have no other Gods before me,
was the most important one.
But, it's been lost like all the rest. A crisis has begun.

Thou shalt not bear false witness
or covet thy neighbor's wife.
These words are so important but,
like the others, they have died.

Keep the Sabbath holy. On this day you should rest.
Can't we find one day a week, our Master's name to bless?

Do not take the Lord, thy God's precious name in vain.
Some forget that this was written
and curse Him just the same.

God could have left a thousand but,
He gave us only ten.
Is it really too much to ask to remember them,
now and then?

We wouldn't have this problem if we'd listen from the start.
And taken the Ten Commandments
and written them in our hearts.

TOO MUCH TO DO

You asked the Lord for a blessing today but,
what for Him did you do?
You cooked, cleaned and watched TV
till the day was almost through.

Then you fed your husband and kids
while your Bible sat on a shelf.
You did a lot for others but, nothing for yourself.

Then, so tired and exhausted in the bed you lay.
It's time to talk to God but, fall asleep as you pray.

Then morning comes and you need help again.
God's name you call.
But, the laundry is piled up to the ceiling
and you have to wash it all.

Then your day is repeated, just like the day before.
No matter how much you do,
there always seems to be more.

Then one day, you're all alone.
Your house is clean and your kids are all grown.

You cry to God and say; I'm ready for You.
He replies, I'm sorry. I have too much to do.

ALWAYS ONE WITNESS

Remember when you told that lie
and thought that no one knew?
You thought that you got by with it,
but God, he knew the truth.

What about the time you schemed
and planned to hurt someone?
The only one you hurt was you
because God sees all that's done.

Did you think it was funny when you stole and got away?
Well, you escaped that time
but you won't on judgment day.

Don't ever be so foolish to think that no one sees.
Because God sees all and you can bet,
you'll get your penalty.

So, try to do what is good and right.
For there are no secrets to him.
Always keep your conscience clean
and don't let the Devil tempt.

When you think you've never lost
and by doing wrong, you've won.
Remember, there's always one witness
who'll make sure justice is done.

TO BE A LITTLE CHILD

To be a little child like me is lonesome in a way,
cause Mom and Dad don't have the time
to come outside and play.

Why are they so busy? Why do they worry so?
They don't even notice me. They will miss as I grow.

I have so many, many dreams I'd like to talk about
but, when I try to tell them they just say please go out.

They don't even know about
the real brave things I've done,
Like hunting lions and tigers with only a BB gun.

Or the time I swam the Pacific Ocean
and got attacked by sharks.
I even killed a grizzly bear and I was back home by dark.

I know my parents love me. I can see it in their eyes.
They are always right beside me when they hear me cry.

But, I think Mom and Dad should
share more things with me,
cause one day I'll be all grown up
and won't fit on my Daddy's knee.

But, as for now I guess I'll keep my secrets to myself.
But, when Mom and Dad can find
the time I sure have lots to tell.

THE LASTING BOOK

I've been pushed aside and rejected,
but also loved and protected.

I've been abused by many and thrown away by some,
but I have always lasted and my work is always done.

I've been burned, torn and mistreated,
but I've never been defeated.

To some I'm nothing, to others I'm all
and I have great power to be so small.

I'm filled with wisdom from beginning to end.
I'm pure, sweet and good.
I cause no harm to anyone.
I never have nor would.

I'm filled with suffering, torture, and pain.
I'm filled with joy and tears.
I'm filled with love and miracles.
I've lived for many years.

I know you're wondering who I am
and how I can be so great,
to only offer peace and love and not one bit of hate.

Well, all I've said is true, and of me I'm sure you've heard
because, dear friend, I'm the Bible
and I hold for you, God's word.

CHAPTER THREE
Prophecy

The Return was written about a year before the September eleventh tragedy. It is the only message that woke me up from a deep sleep in the middle of the night. I tried to put off writing it down till morning but, the Holy Spirit kept saying, NOW! I took the tablet from beside my bed and began to write the things He was telling me. When I finished, I was afraid and crying uncontrollably. To me, it is the most powerful revelation I have ever received.

I received a phone call on that dreadful day in September. It was from my friend and former employer, Gloria. She was terrified and told me to turn on my TV to look at what had just happened. She said that I had predicted the tragedy with the poem that God had given me. I denied it and it had not entered my mind. So, after I hung up the phone, I went and read the poem again. I thought it could have been a prediction. It would be a few years later, after the tsunami devastation before I realized it really was a prediction. I had taken the poem as a whole, about the return of our Lord. Then I realized it was broken down into several different events leading to His return. Regardless of the interpretation, it will definitely move you. You be the judge.

THE RETURN

The day was just beginning, not a cloud in the sky.
Everyone was just as busy
with their normal routines of life.

No one was expecting the events
that would soon take place,
until the storm clouds gathered
and disrupted the peaceful day.

The earth began to tremble and the buildings began to fall.
People began to panic and fear consumed them all.

Thunder crashed and the lightning flashed
and the wind uprooted the trees.
The rain poured as never before
and water flooded the streets.

Cars collided, houses collapsed and sirens
were screaming around town.
There were several explosions and waves left the oceans
and thousands of people were drowned.

There was mass confusion. No one could think.
Many thought this was the end.
Others cried God and fell on their knees
and began to repent of their sins.

He wasn't listening to their cries anymore,
a lesson they all soon learned.
For, He was too busy fulfilling his promise
and preparing for His return.

All at once, the sky split wide open
and the people were begging to die.
But death could not relieve them,
as the Lamb of God had arrived.

A cloud appeared and the Son of Man
descended toward the earth.
Every eye was upon him as he slowly began to emerge.

I believe a few started screaming,
oh Lord, have mercy on me.
Others just stood there trembling,
too terrified to speak.

They had no peace or comfort,
not one woman nor one man.
They knew they would suffer eternally,
as they cursed the mark on their hands.

Judgment was upon them.
What were they going to do?
God was real, after all and the Bible really was true.

MOTHER EARTH

The earth is having birth pains more frequent every day.
We hear her cries from destruction, disasters and dismay.

She's increased with crime and violence.
Oh, the time is near
for Mother Earth to deliver a time of pain and fear.

For God said, in the Bible, notice all these things,
for they tell you that I am near and judgment will I bring.

Now, it's true we've always had theses things;
murders, crimes and war.
But I think you will agree,
there's more now than ever before.

That's why God said birth pains. So, that we would know.
Because as they get closer, the climax must unfold.

So this you can be sure of, no matter how you scorn,
the day is almost here when horror, shall be born.

FALSE PROPHETS

Question every spirit, whether it be of me.
Because they appear holy, doesn't mean they can't deceive.

Many shall come in my name,
proclaiming they're prophets of God.
But don't believe every word they say,
for disciples they are not.

Satan has many powers and angels that do his will.
They walk among the midst of you,
and churches as well are filled.

They take my words and add their own,
distracting you from the truth.
You don't see the harm they cause
for the act like they worship, too.

If they told you they were evil
and they were leading you astray.
Then, you'd know for certain
and you'd turn and walk away.

So, they cover themselves with honey
and their words are sincere and sweet.
They even read the bible and preach but, it is not for Me.

So, when someone gets your interest
by talking about Me or my word,
don't be eager to believe them for they can make your
problems worse.

I've given you the power to understandthe word yourself.
but listen to your heart and
not the words from someone else.

When you worship, keep an open mind
and be aware at all times
that the person sitting right next to could be Satan,
in disguise.

FINAL WARNING

The end of time is coming but, no one will believe
that we're living in the latter days but, only a few can see.

The signs are in the heavens on earth and in God's words.
But people seem so blinded
and closed ears have never heard.

Throughout the entire Bible are examples of such things.
The warnings were ignored but judgment always came.

The people of Sodom and Gomorah
thought it was all a joke.
But everyone laughed at Noah
as they watched him build his boat.

Through the years, God has proven
that what he says will be done.
Only the ones who listen are the ones who overcome.

Behold I come quickly, is the message He's giving now.
The sky will open as a scroll and He'll appear on a cloud.

So remember, how it's been in the past,
before you start to scorn.
For, I know the next knock I hear may be Jesus at my door.

MY CHILDREN

All my children are talking about what they are going to do,
as evil totally engulfs the earth
and Satan makes them confused.

I've told them all about him
and everything there is to know.
Still their hearts are troubled,
their eyes and ears remain closed.

They refuse to heed my warning
and I knew this day would come.
They only have to look to Me.
Then, they'll know what must be done.

The time is drawing near and Satan has little time.
So, he's using every trick he has to try
and take what's mine.

Soon, I must send my judgments
and plagues upon the earth.
Then you'll know what fear really is
and you'll curse the day of your birth.

You'll wish they had listened but,
for some it will be too late.
You'll even take this mark of Satan,
believing it's not a mistake.

I am the Lord, thy God and I can make the mountains fall.
I can shake the stars out of heaven
and I will ignore you when you call.

Messages From God

I will turn my back on you as you've turned theirs on me.
Wake up my children and see the light,
before this day of grief.

Confess your sins and open your hearts
and I'll guide you every step of the way
or be afraid and follow him,
right in through hell's burning gates.

WHERE IS PEACE?

Everyone is crying peace, but peace will never be,
unless we learn to rid the world of sin, lust and greed.

We don't know the secret to rid the world of these.
So then my friend, I hope you see,
that we shall have no peace.

There will always be one who says;
I'm rich but I want more.
There will always be just one more man
who craves the greed of war.

And one will always hold within a cruel
and hardened heart.
One will always search and find another fight to start.

Until our Lord returns again, we shall have no peace.
Only He is great enough, to perform such a wondrous deed.

So, if it's really peace we want then we must look to Him,
to keep our spirits lifted high
and our lights from growing dim.

Peace on earth is needed, but God frees us from our sins.
So, the peace that is most important
is the peace that lies within.

REVELATIONS

As I watch the TV and listen to the news,
I know our days on earth are very, very, few.

When I read the paper, its pages are filled with crime.
Everyone had better believe, we're running out of time.

You see, God gave a message
of the things which are to come
in the book of Revelations, chapters 1 through 21.

He tells us of the earthquakes and the gold and silver craze.
If you'd take time to read this book,
I'm sure you'd be amazed.

You say you are a Christian and you live the Christian way;
Yet you are not concerned with what this book has to say.

Some people say, that it's old news,
these things have all been done.
But, chapter 1 and verse 19,
say the things which are to come.

If the book of Revelations was something of the past,
then, why wasn't it the first book and not the very last?

It takes a little research to understand this book.
Most of you don't have the time
or you're just afraid to look.

Well, here's some news for you,
a true Christian is not afraid,
because to see his Savior is a blessed, blessed day.

So please, read Revelations,
and when you do, you'll understand
that the main thing it tells you is the end is at hand.

THE ANTICHRIST

The book of Revelations tells us of a man,
who's called the great deceiver
and he'll come to spoil our land.

He'll make a lot of promises
and perform for us great deeds.
He'll say that he is God himself,
and he can fill our needs.

He'll tell us of his power.
He'll tell us of his plans.
We must receive a mark
on our foreheads or our hands.

If we take this mark of his, we'll be doomed forever more,
because God has gave us warnings
that should not be ignored.

If we refuse to take this mark and choose to die instead.
Then, we'll get a home in paradise
for believing in what God said.

This man is really Satan; he'll be called the antichrist
and all the things he has to say are really skillful lies.

I know these things I say are true just
as I know the night is dark.
I pray that you believe them too
or you might receive the mark.

JUDGMENT DAY

Will you smile on judgment day or will you wear a frown?
Will you just get ashes or will you get a crown?

Will God look at you and say; no treasures have you won?
Or will he look at you and say;
your job has been well done?

Will you shake and tremble?
Will your heart be filled with fear?
Will your soul be troubled?
Will your eyes be filled with tears?

Will you be rejoicing and calling out his name?
Will you be unhappy? Will you be ashamed?

Maybe, you never think about what you'll do that day
or how you will act or feel, or what you're going to say?

Will you have eternal life or will your soul be doomed?
It's something you should think about
because it's coming soon.

CHAPTER FOUR

Comfort

THE DAY WE MEET

God almighty, I sometimes think about the day we meet.
My mind can't even begin to absorb the beauty that I'll see.

The thought of meeting our wondrous Lord,
and thank him face to face
for giving me His mercy, His love and His grace.

To tell you that I'm thankful for all the things You've done.
Although I have had some heart aches,
You've mended every one.

And though I've cried my share of tears,
you've always dried my eyes,
and every time I felt I was lost,
you kept me in your sight.

I want to tell You how much
I've enjoyed living on Your earth.
Having a chance to love and be loved
and for my baby's birth.

Having a son made me realize
how much a heart could love.
You nailed Yours to a cross for me.
How could we ever thank you enough?

My list of thanks is endless and it makes me stop and think
about the greatest gift of all, to live forever with the King.

ALL DRESSED UP

There's a body of a man in a casket colored blue.
He's all dressed up, so perfect, in one of his finest suits.

The flowers are arriving and one by one, they are placed.
to brighten up the room where his family awaits.

As I looked upon him, I noticed how he had changed.
He had a glow around him. His face showed no pain.

Cause there's a soul of a man in heaven looking down.
He has been freed of the misery that once had him bound.

Although we're going to miss him,
I wouldn't want him to return
to the life that he was living here with us on earth.

For I know he's happy in the Master's loving arms.
That's where he'll never again be lonely
or suffer a broken heart.

That's where everyday he'll wake up
smiling and it never has to end.
The Lord will be his comfort
and the angels will be his friends.

So, why should I cry and worry
when I know these things are true?
If we want him to have the best,
then the best dear Lord, is with you.

In memory of D.J. Blair, he was killed in a tragic car accident at the age of three. The day of his funeral was a rainy Sunday afternoon. He spoke to me from heaven and inspired me to write this poem. I wrote what I heard and it somehow eased my pain, as I hope it will ease yours too.

A GIFT FROM GOD

I once was an angel, who lived upon the earth.
I was loved so deeply by everyone at birth.

But, my Father who is in heaven had a purpose to fulfill.
I had to leave my earthly home because it was His will.

Those of you I left behind will never understand.
He wanted me to leave as a child
before I knew the sins of man.

The reason I was so special, not an ordinary child,
was because I was loaned to you, from heaven for a while.

When I entered into his kingdom,
as you all know I have done,
I felt blessed and thankful that I was a chosen one.

I was so pure, sweet and innocent,
without a flaw against my soul.
Being so perfect and so beautiful got me my crown of gold.

So, remember me forever and what I meant to you.
Be thankful for this gift from God
that He chose to share with you.

YOUR FRIEND

So, you say you're unhappy, confused and alone.
All of your good times are already gone.
Nobody loves you. Nobody cares.
Your load is too heavy and too great to bear.

Well, listen my child, lend me your ear.
You've not a worry and you've not a fear.
So, wipe your tears and stand up tall.
For, you have a friend after all.

You have the world in the palm of your hand.
Cause your friend's love will forever stand.

Your friend's love is always there.
Your friend's love is everywhere.
Your one friend is the beginning and end;
all your burdens, He will mend.

You say you can't see Him or walk by His side,
or cry on his shoulder when you want to hide.
You say you don't know Him, not even His name.
and he can love you is not really plain.

I'll give you His name and never think twice.
Cause your friend is my friend, our Lord Jesus Christ.

THE MIGHTY HAND

Lord, I have much fear of you,
though I know your love is true.

For I know the power You hold within,
by watching You guide the raging wind.

I hear your voice in thunder and it makes me tremble so.
To know that I have ever sinned against
One who is so bold.

Just one lift of Your smallest finger
and all evil You could destroy.
Yet, You show us mercy and give to us such joy.

You've showed Your love so many ways,
mainly with your Son.
Oh Lord, why are we so foolish
to have done the things we've done

Lord, it's true, I fear you, but only because I should.
Lord, I'm so thankful that You're a God so good.

Lord, You said when you returned,
that some would beg to die.
My Father, who art in heaven, I pray that it's not I.

THANK YOU FOR THE CHILDREN

Thank you for the children Lord,
that make our lives worthwhile,
because even when we're at our worst,
a child can make us smile.

The do and say a lot of things that we don't understand,
but Lord you sure put magic
in the touch of their little hands.

You put some sunshine in their face,
and you put the stars in their eyes.
You even added a little rain, so that they could cry.

The sweet and tender love they give
could only come from You,
and a little child shows your grace
and mercy through and through.

Though sometimes they wan too much
and have too many needs,
thank you for the children Lord and for giving one to me.

I LOOKED UP

I looked up in the sky today and guess what all I saw.
I saw a rainbow dancing by. What else can I recall?

I saw a cloud so pretty it took my breath away.
I saw the big and mighty sun and felt its lovely rays.

I looked up in the sky last night and guess what all I saw.
I saw the glory of the moon, I saw a star so small.

I saw a lot of beauty that lives in all that space,
and all the beauty I saw is part of the Master's face.

CHAPTER FIVE
Strength

GOLD WATCH AND CHAIN

The winter wind was blowing
and the snow was falling down.
I was on my way to church
when I saw something on the ground.

When I stooped down to pick it up,
what it was, was very plain.
I was holding in my hand an old gold watch and chain.

I dropped it in my pocket and turned around to go.
Then that's when I saw him,
half covered with freezing snow.

I rushed over to him, but he was barely alive.
I knew he wouldn't last very long
cause he was at least seventy-five.

I took my coat and covered him.
Then I asked, what was his name.
But, the only words I understood
were about a watch and chain.

I told him I had found it, as I raised up his head.
Then, he tried to talk again, and this is what he said;
Son, I know I'm dying and there's nothing you can do.
I'm too old and tired to fight so,
please listen until I'm through.

That old gold watch you've found isn't worth an awful lot.
But, I need an offering for church today
and that is all I've got.

You see, God says to give and then we shall receive.
So, will you take it to the church?
It would mean so much to me.

The old man didn't notice that I'd began to cry.
He looked up at me and smiled
and the then the old man died.

When I walked into the church, every head looked my way.
And I know they were wondering why I was so late.

I didn't say a word about
what had happened to me that day.
I just took out that gold watch and chain
and dropped it in the offering plate.

ANGELS UNAWARE

Our Lord is coming soon,
she said as she walked along the street.
She had no coat to warm her and no shoes upon her feet.

The crowd was rushing by her too busy to hear her words.
But I walked up closer because of what I'd heard.

Ma'am, I said to her, they're not listening to what you say.
Why don't you just go on home? It's such a dreadful day.

She looked at me with tears in her eyes
and said it's not all in vain
because although they pass me by,
you chose to remain.

You see, each day I walk these streets
and preach about the good news.
The crowd is always larger, but the ones who stop are few.

I have no home to go to and I have no bed at night.
I find rest is anywhere, when you're guided by the light.

The Holy Spirit leads me and I know that He'll provide.
My job is to tell others, whether they listen or pass me by.

May God bless you for stopping and giving me your time.
You don't know how it pleases me
or how it eases my mind.

I watched her walk away in the freezing snow and rain.
Then, I began to follow her, for I hadn't asked her name.

She went into an alley and I was very close behind.
But, when I got to where she was,
the woman I could not find.

It seemed as though she disappeared right before my eyes.
I stood there looking helpless and staring at the sky.

I felt a chill go over me while I was standing there.
As I remembered what the Bible
says about angels unaware.

OPEN HEART

When I open up my eyes, there are so many things to see.
I'm so thankful for my sight, the good Lord gave to me.

When I open up my ears, I hear so many things,
the sounds of love that fill the air.
What happiness hearing brings.

But, when I open up my heart, that's the greatest gift of all,
because it makes me love the world
and all creatures, great and small.

A heart that's soft and honest and as pure as gold,
is the greatest treasure, that anyone can hold.

If I had no sight, my heart would be my eyes.
And though I'd live in darkness, I'd also live in the light.

If I had no hearing, my heart would be my ears.
And though I'd live in silence, I would also hear.

But, if I was to close my heart,
even though I could see and hear,
I would really be deaf and blind and always live in fear.

Yes, I'm thankful for my eyes
and ears and every other part,
but most of all, I'm thankful for my open heart.

GET BEHIND ME SATAN

Get behind me Satan. I have no need for you.
For there's nothing you can offer me
but things I cannot use.

I'm aware that you have power, for you use it everyday.
I see the damage that you do and the ones you lead astray.

Your prey is little children and spirit-weakened minds.
Souls that are lost and troubled are the ones you like to find.

Satan, you are nothing but tricks, schemes and lies.
You are oh, so foolish for thinking that you're wise

It's true that you have power,
but there's One who's greater still.
You cannot do anything, unless it is to be His will.

So, get behind me Satan, for I serve the One that's true.
I serve the living lasting God, so there's no room for you.

DO YOU EVER PRAY?

I was talking to a friend about the troubles that she had.
I'll admit that what she said really sounded bad.

As I sat there listening to what she had to say.
I looked at her with tear filled eyes
and asked if she had prayed.

She looked at me so funny and said, I never pray.
All I do is worry about what problems
I'll have the next day.

I said child, no wonder you're in the shape you're in.
What do you expect from life without God,
your only friend?

She said, who do you think you are to talk to me this way?
Because, you have no troubles and you're happy every day.

I said, yes I'm happy my life is filled with joy.
I have a lot of blessings and a darling little boy.

I have a life that's filled with love,
that's what I've been trying to say.
The reason that I have so much is because I pray.

3/17
300
u/s

Dunbar
feb 4
8AM

284 5887

Rad.
781
4000
Baptist East films